Signs

by Judy Ker

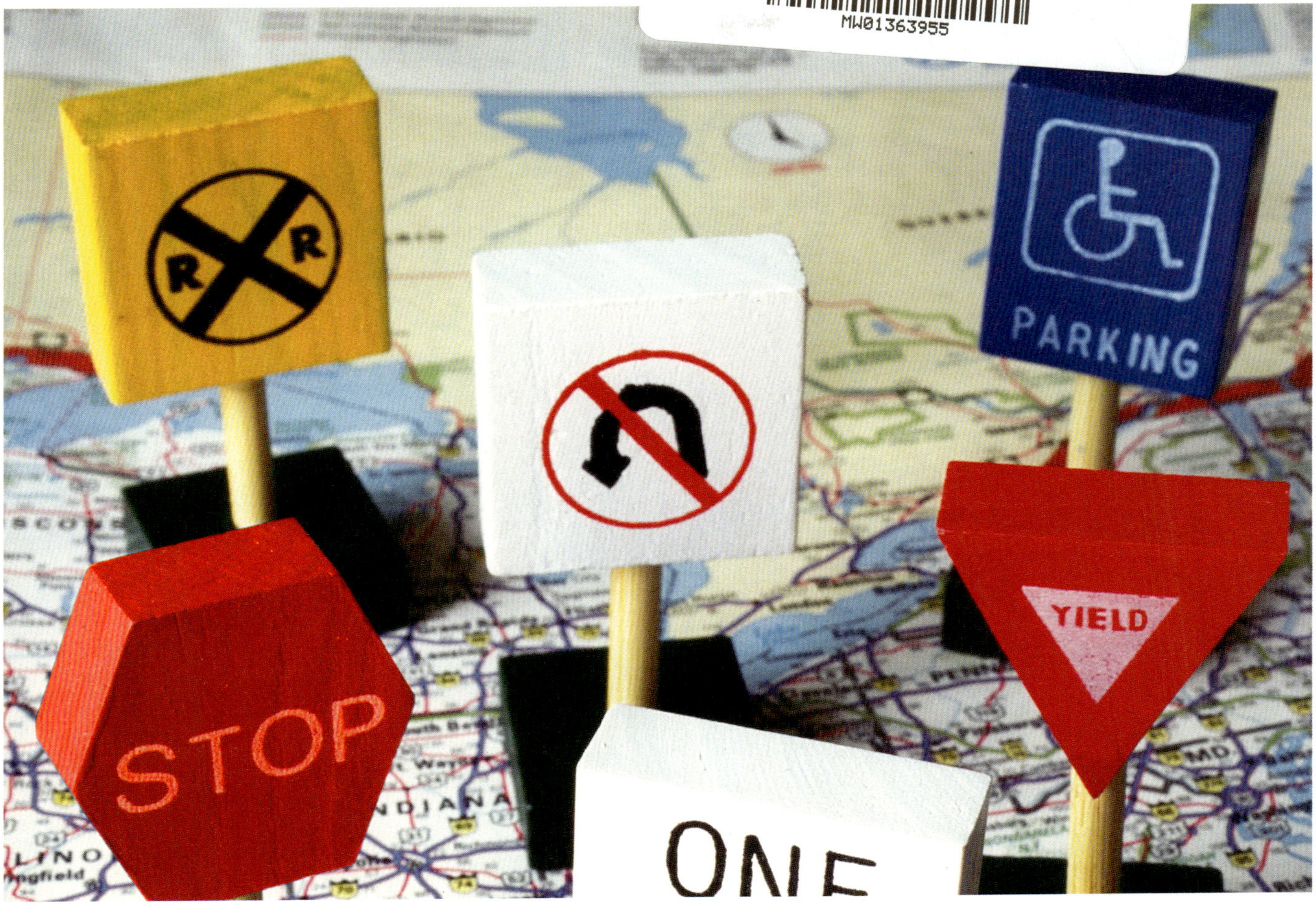

I see the 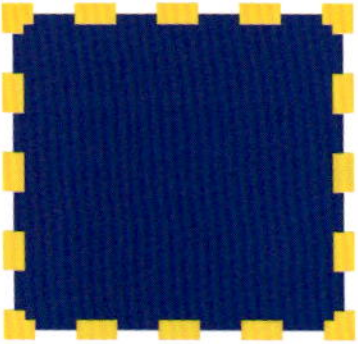 .

square

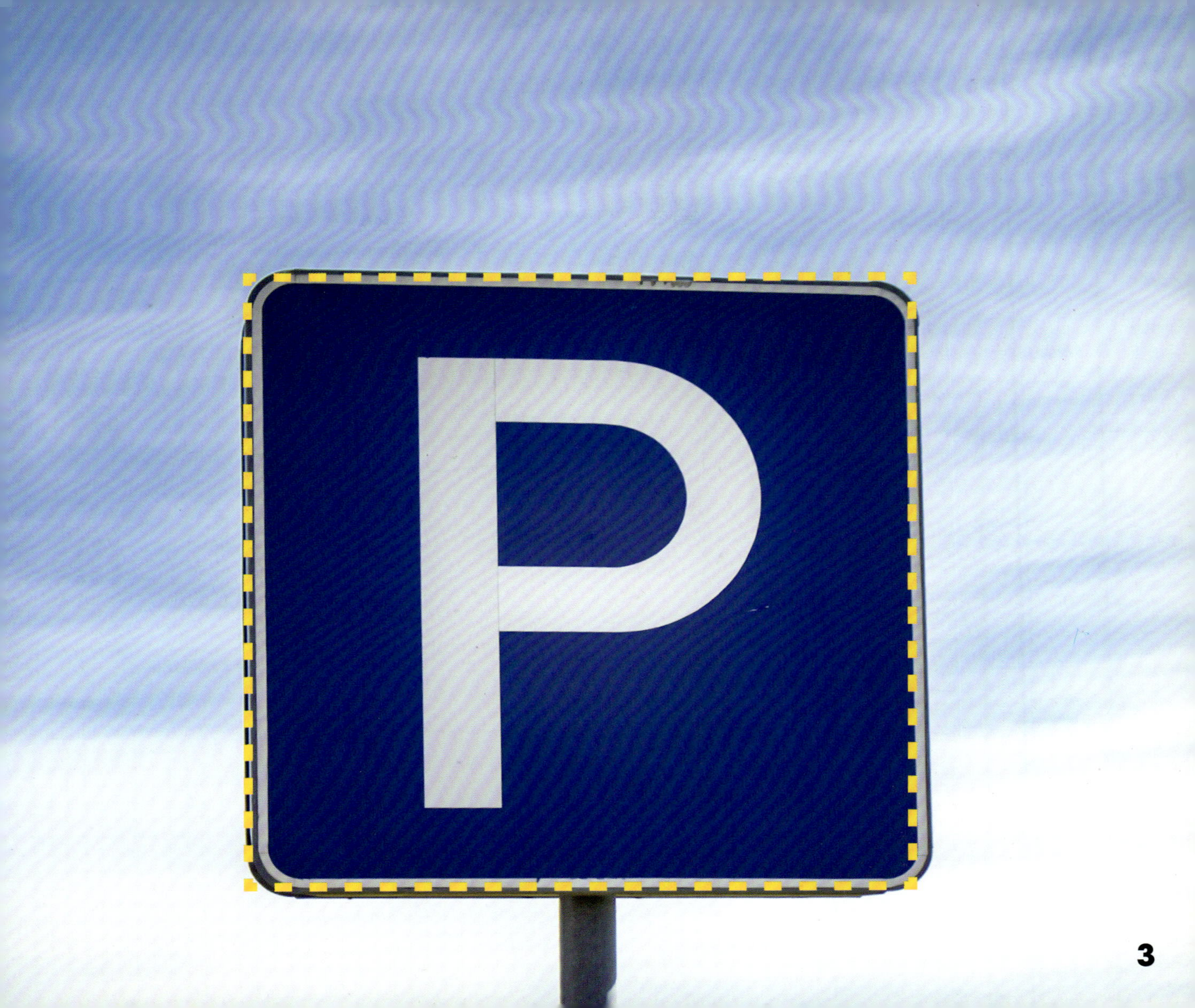
P

I see the 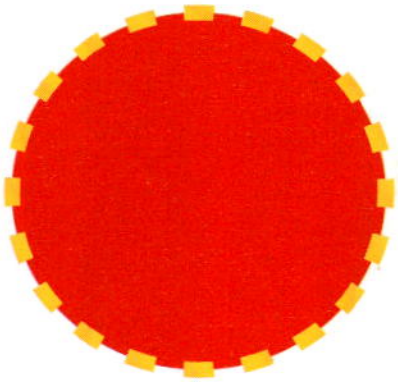 .

circle

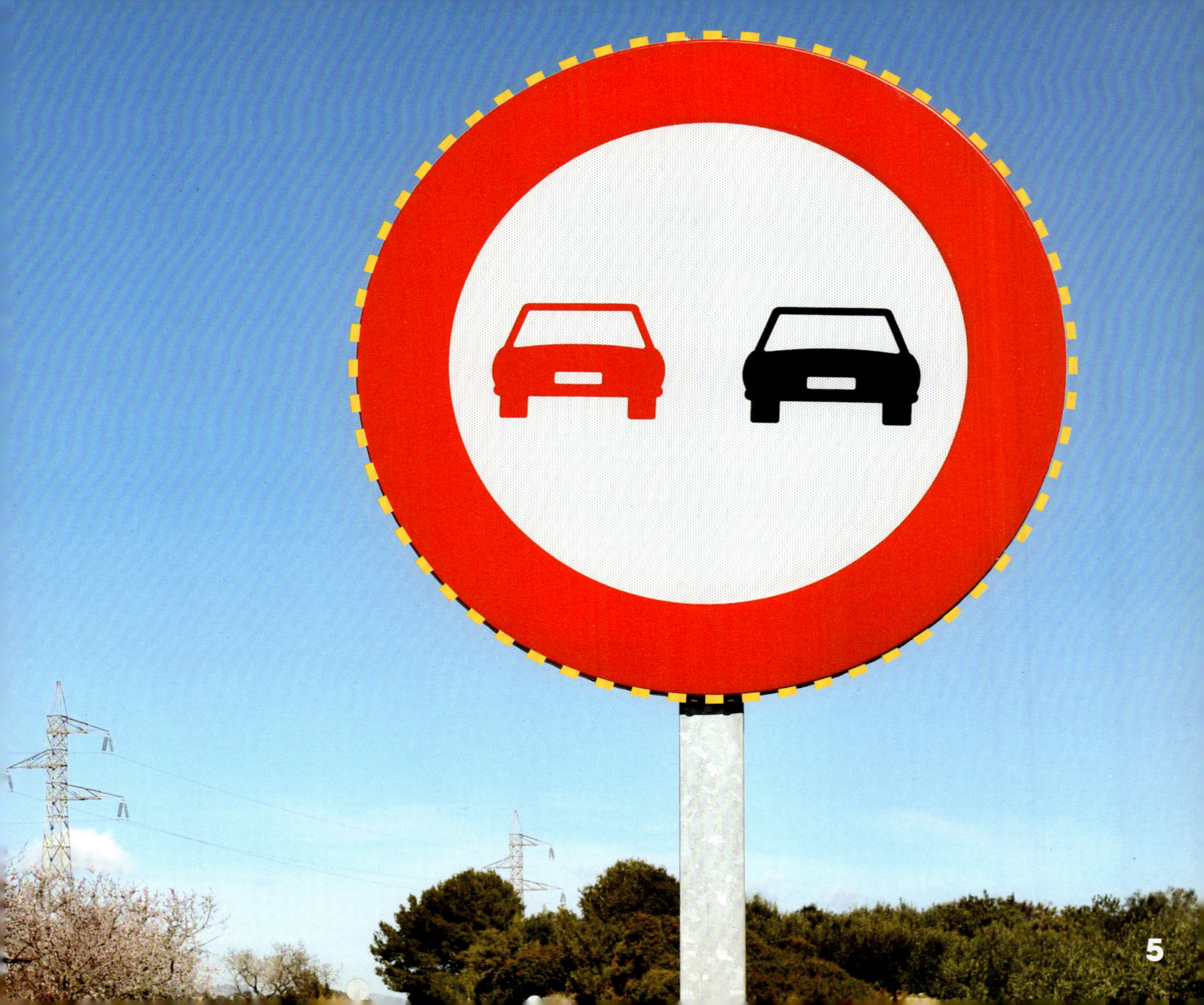

I see the 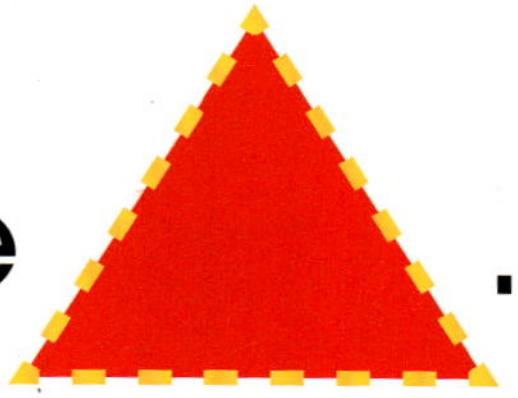 .

triangle

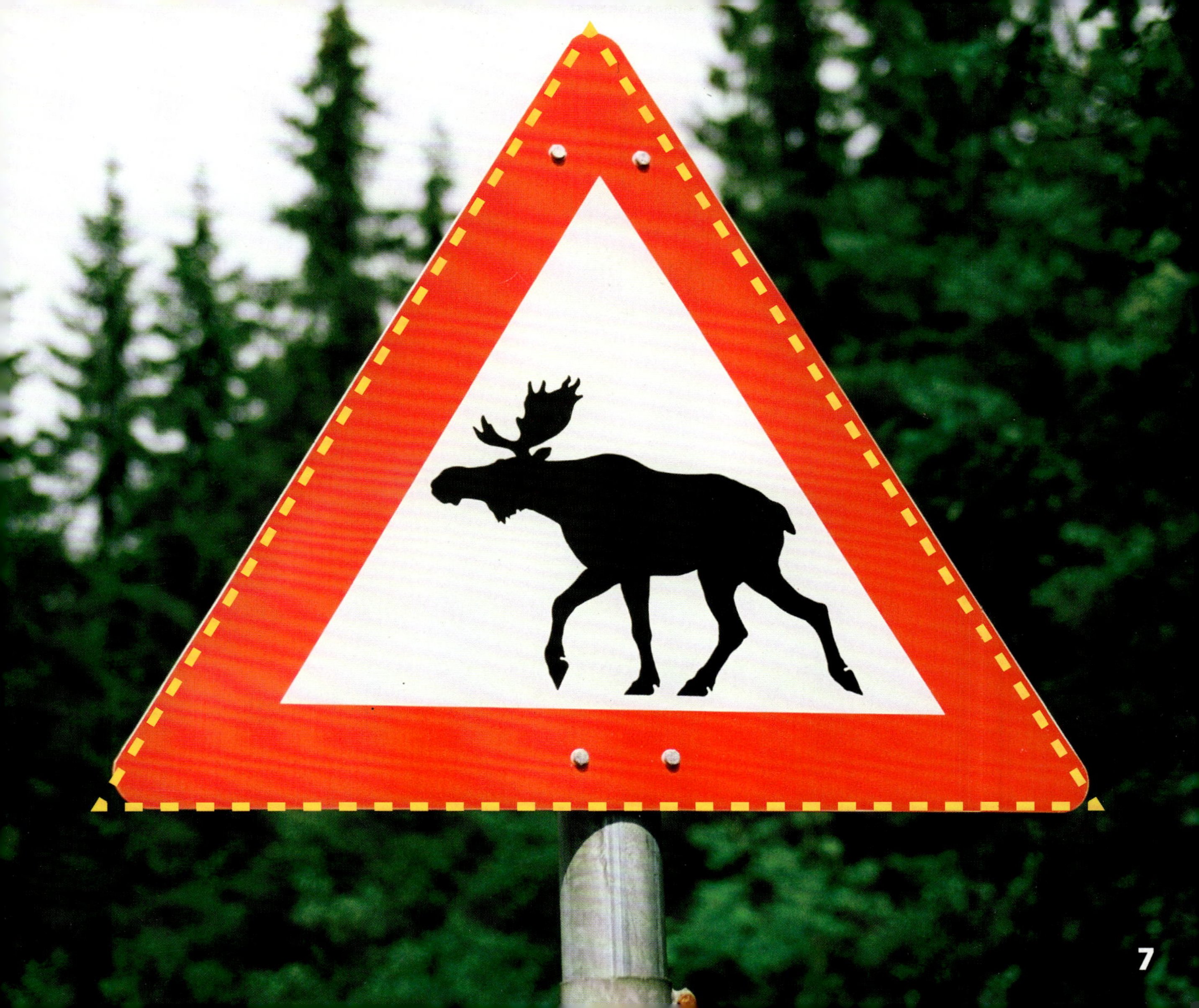

I see the 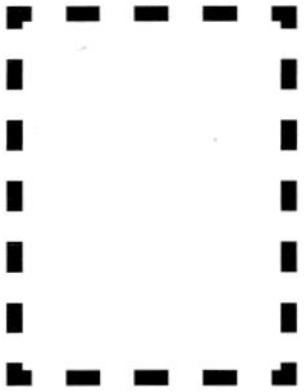 .

rectangle

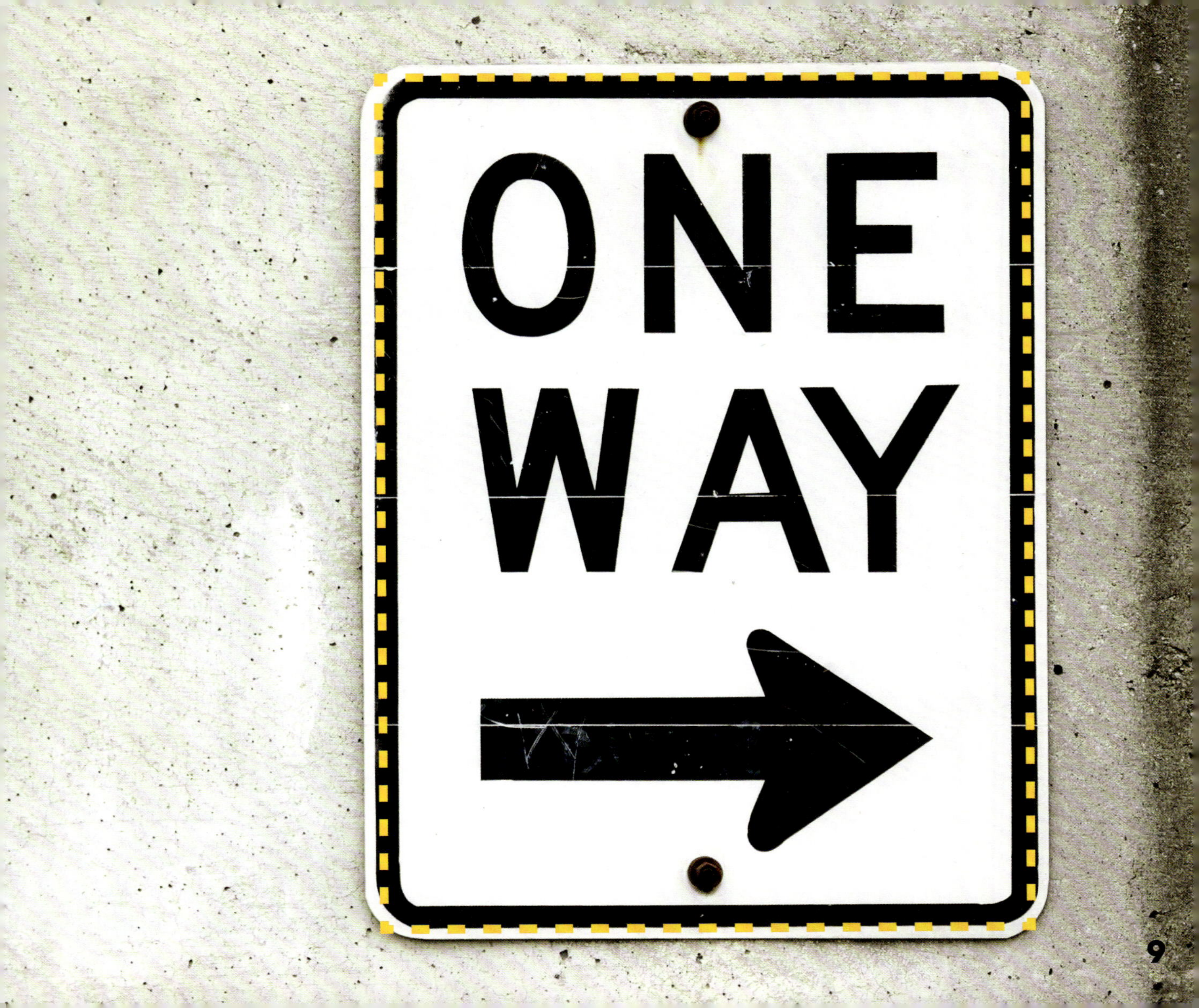
ONE
WAY

I see the 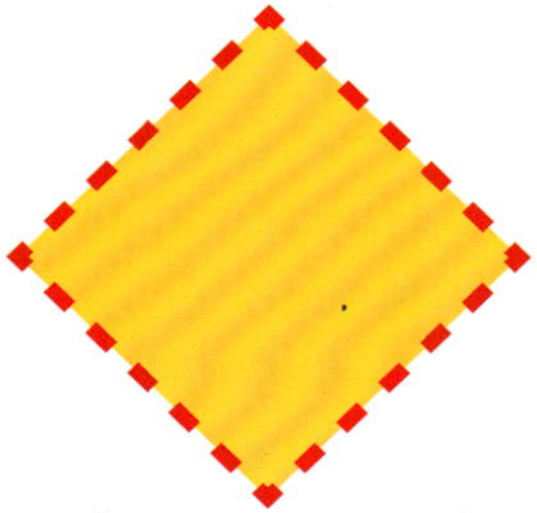 .

diamond

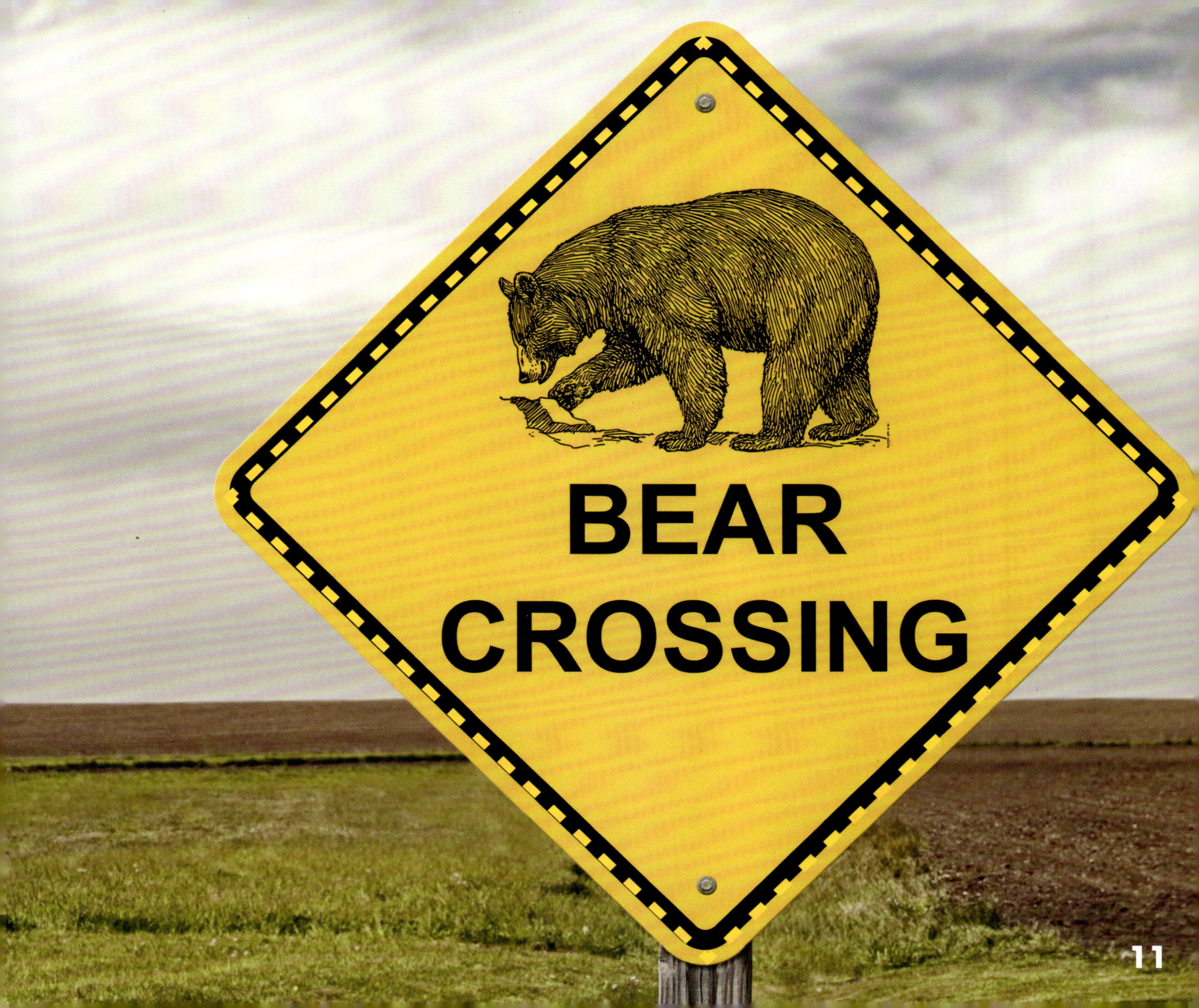
BEAR
CROSSING

I see the 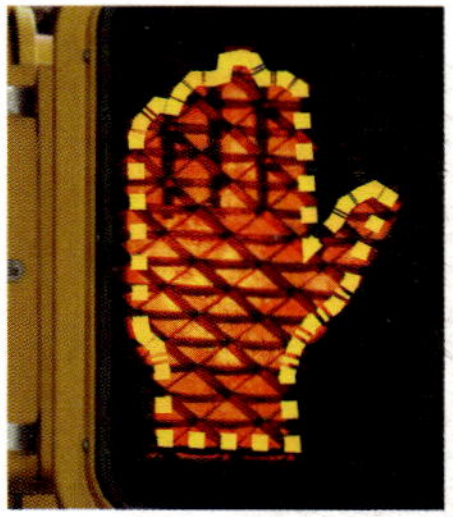 .

hand

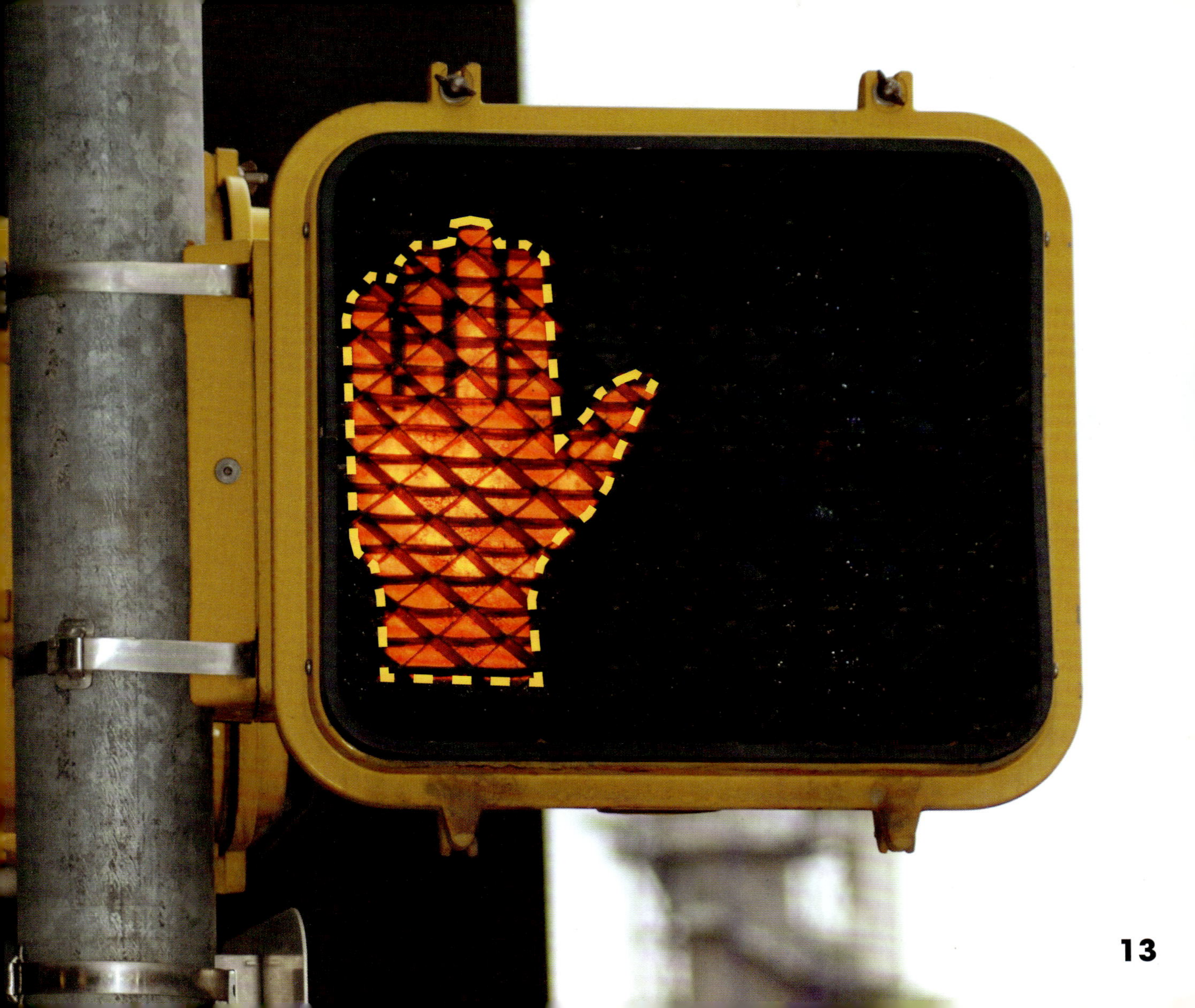

I see the 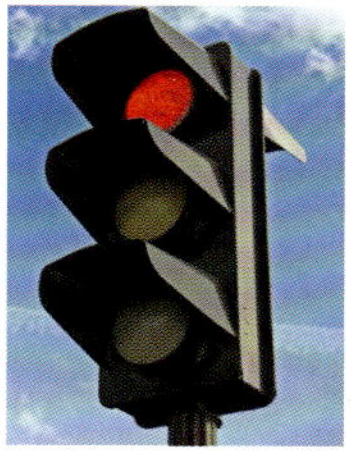 .

stoplight

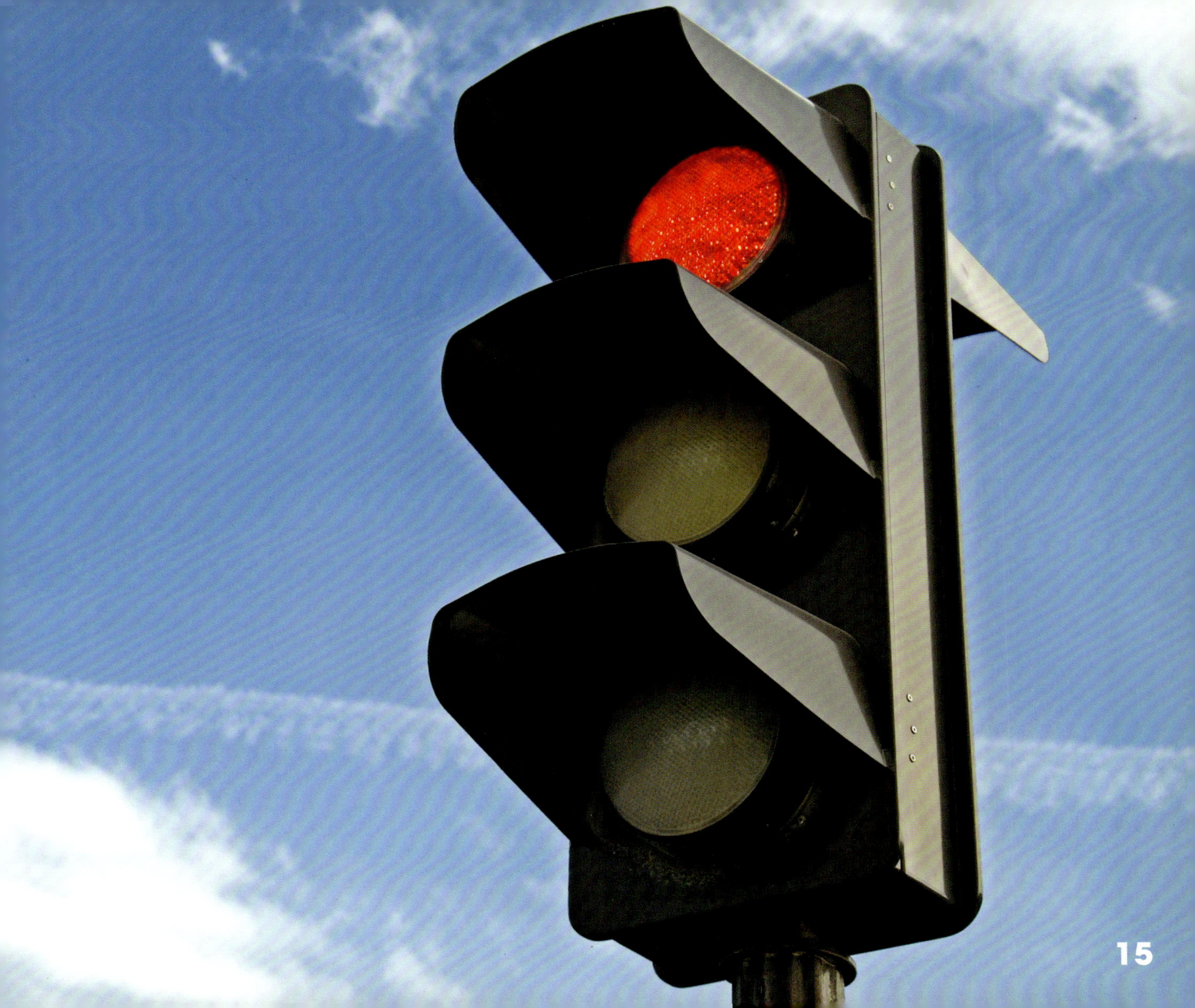

I see the 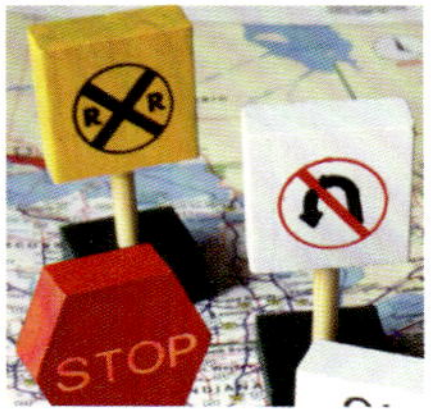 .

signs

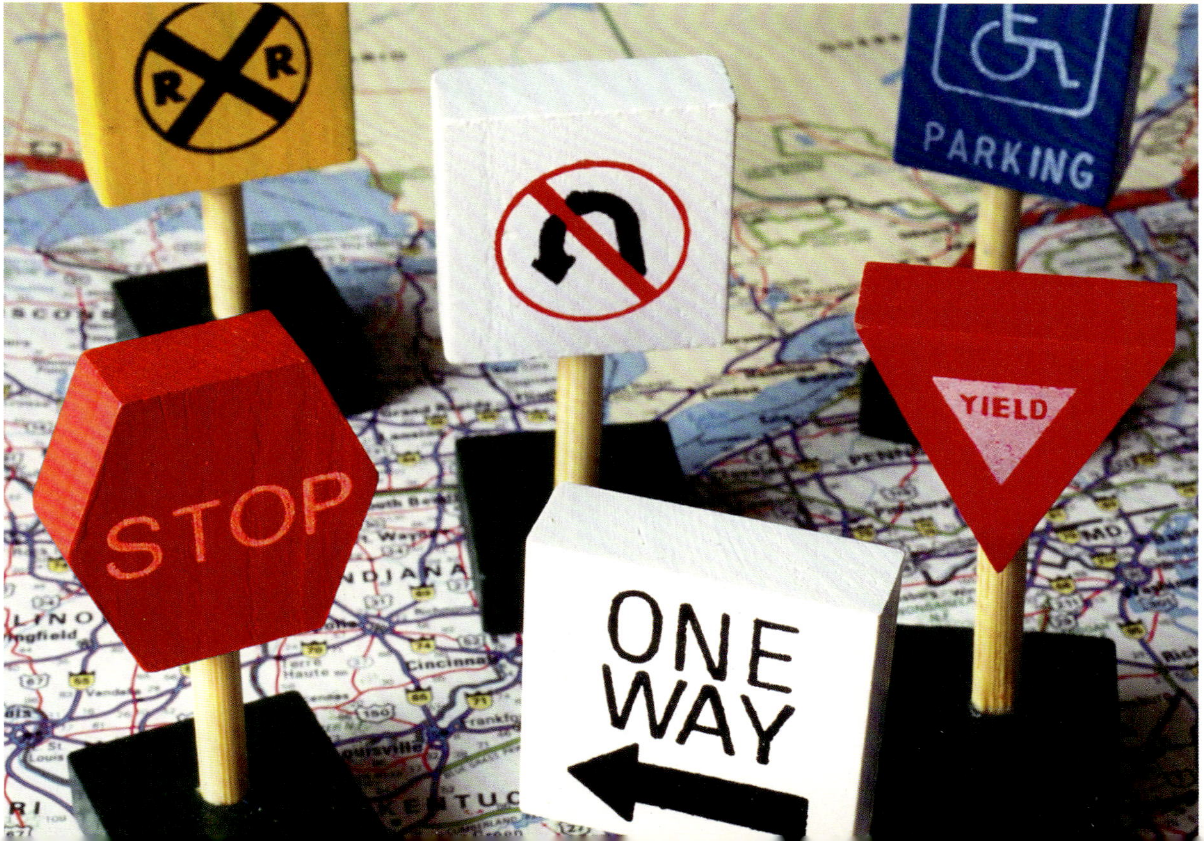